T0041139

THE ULTIMATE **Music Assessment and Evaluation** KIT

FOR THE GENERAL MUSIC TEACHER

Practical Strategies, Time-Saving Tips, Samples, Forms and More

By Cheryl Lavender

I gratefully acknowledge my talented colleague in music education, Sue Broker, of Swanson Elementary School, Brookfield, Wisconsin, who helped develop, field-test and refine many of the assessment strategies offered herein, and without whose support and encouragement this project would not have been possible.

7777 W. BLUEMOUND RD. P.O. BOX 13819 MILWAUKEE, WI 53213

TABLE OF CONTENTS

TRODUCTION

"I believe that arts education—music education—should be its own reward. However, the reality is, and this is the message I want to leave with you, is that that's not going to be enough anymore. In education in this country, and in education in other parts of the world, there's tremendous competition for time and resources. If you're not accountable, if you can't demonstrate that your kids are learning something that's important, you aren't even in the conversation."

– Howard Gardner,
IKS/OAKE Kodaly Symposium/Conference, Hartford, CT, August, 1993

Mincing few words, Howard Gardner (co-director of ARTSPropel) asserts that accountability for music education is here to stay. If music is to be a valid, core academic subject like math and science, then the study of music must also be measured, documented and evaluated. Although teacher training for music assessment is on the rise, it has been found that many assessment models being used are more suitable for *music performance groups* than for *general music class.* With hundreds of students and little prep time, general music teachers are heroically (and frantically) inventing their own music assessment prototypes every day. And, knowing *what, when* and *how* to assess is still at best, confusing.

It's hard to imagine a *one-size-fits-most* model for assessing children's musical development in the K-8 general music classroom. However, ***The Ultimate Music Assessment and Evaluation Kit*** attempts to offer you, the general music teacher, just that. This kit is the result of years of sheer trial and error with research and studies of best practices from many successful general music programs. The enclosed user-friendly assessment components have been developed, field-tested and refined for use with over 2000 elementary and middle school students since 1994 in the School District of Elmbrook, Brookfield, Wisconsin.

This kit is designed to be entirely flexible and adaptable. Assessment components are included to meet *most* general music assessment needs from the least elaborate to the most comprehensive of assessment requirements. Inside you'll find practical strategies, time-saving tips, assessment samples, ready-to-assemble forms and more. With these tools at your fingertips, you can custom design your own assessment and evaluation method that best suits your teaching style while meeting the needs of your music program.

Even with hundreds of students and a tightly-packed schedule, assessment and evaluation in the general music classroom *can* be manageable (without more frowns or grey hairs)! So, knowing that much of the work with music assessment is already done, take a deep breath, let go of the stress, and *enjoy* music teaching!

– Cheryl Lavender

EVALUATING CHILDREN'S MUSICAL DEVELOPMENT IN THE GENERAL MUSIC CLASSROOM—
WHATS WRONG WITH THE *OLD* WAY?

Uh-oh...report card time! With hundreds of music students and not enough time to really know them, doing report card grades is definitely a pain. Let's see ... Michael listens well, sits up straight, is cooperative—music grade: B. LaQuita sings beautifully, takes private violin lessons, and her father is principal clarinetist in the symphony—if that's not an A, nothing is! Then there's Billy. He has dirty clothes, is frequently absent, can't sit still—music grade: C.

Before the dawn of music assessment, a child's music grade was quite often the music teacher's subjective judgment of that child's effort, behavior, or personal attributes. Some music grades were based on attendance and attitude. Musically speaking however, these "qualifiers" had little to do with a child's actual musical development. Sadly, these kinds of criteria enabled music teachers to use the music grade as a reward for compliant, easy-to-teach children, or as a punishment for behaviorally-challenged or learning-resistive children. In any case, because music grades of the past often reflected *non-musical* criteria, they were not the most meaningful, accurate or fair reflectors of children's actual musical development. It's no wonder that music programs were viewed as "academically soft" or as "frills" in the curriculum - they appeared to offer nothing "substantial" to document.

Music grades of the past often reflected non-musical criteria.

Truth is, throughout the history of music education, music teachers have been in the business of assessing musical learning against a plethora of *musical* criteria. Consider each time a music teacher discerned a student's intonation during singing; or corrected a student's rhythm while sight-reading; or critiqued a student's notation in an original composition; or analyzed a student's report comparing musical styles - that music teacher was doing music assessment. But in the past, what the music teacher didn't have that the math teacher had, was a systematic and credible way to assess, document and evaluate student learning.

Like learning to speak, learning to make music is a developmental process. Unlike other school subjects such as math (primarily *left* brain), children learn to make music using *whole* brain functions. Making music involves complex, higher order neural processes that integrate aural, spatial, logical, linguistic, kinesthetic, and emotional connections. Children acquire musical skills and knowledge over time at diverse rates of learning with varying degrees of accomplishment. And unlike math, it is often difficult to assess and evaluate a child's musical development with a grade that is meaningful, accurate and fair.

As general music teachers well know, evidence of musical learning is mostly seen and heard at a concert. But a concert is one kind of musical learning product. Of greater significance is the ongoing singing, listening, reading, writing, playing, moving, composing, and describing music that occur daily or weekly in the general music classroom. The general music classroom is where music content instruction takes place. It's where the products of musical learning are processed and internalized in the minds and hearts of children. It's where musical growth can be assessed, documented, and evaluated over time—it's where the general music program is truly accountable.

Let's begin with a look at the difference between assessment and evaluation:

- To *assess* is to measure learning and gather data about learning.
- To *evaluate* is to analyze and interpret the learning data in order to make a judgment. The evaluation of a child's musical learning progress is often reported to parents and school in the form of a report card *grade.*

With initiatives like *Goals 2000: Educate America Act* of 1994 (in which the arts were written into law as core subjects in American schools), music educators identified Music Content Standards - *what all students should know and be able to do.* The voluntary *Nine National Standards for Music Education* (Consortium of National Arts Education Associations, Reston, VA: MENC, 1994) became established. (See p. 34.) In 1996, *Performance Standards for Music: Strategies and Benchmarks for Assessing Progress Toward the National Standards* (Reston, VA: MENC), were also developed. State and local districts began to identify their own music standards and specific learner objectives for the general music curriculum. And along with standards came implementation and *music assessment.* Perhaps the most valuable result of all these developments is the birth of a new pedagogical philosophy:

> Like other *core academic subjects,* such as math and science, the study of *music* can be assessed, documented and evaluated.

Like other core academic subjects, the study of music can be assessed, documented and evaluated.

In the general music classroom, it's now recognized that in order to be meaningful, accurate and fair, a grade which reflects children's musical learning progress must be arrived at through a combination of music assessments, such as:

- guided practice sessions
- recorded observations of children making music
- practice pages, assignments, notes, tests, quizzes
- children's personal reflections
- journal writings
- teacher, self and peer assessments
- interviews, surveys and questionnaires
- samples of student work collected over time in portfolios (paper, audio, video or disk)

These types of assessments measure children's musical development against meaningful criteria that over time, show evidence of musical learning growth. Music assessments provide feedback for teacher and student alike. From assessment results, music instruction can be adapted or refined, and students can recognize their learning strengths as well as areas for improvement. At the end of a grading period, the results of music assessments can be tallied, translated into an evaluation, and communicated with a report card grade. When a music grade is based on these kinds of learning evidence, we can then say it is a meaningful, accurate, and fair reflector of children's actual musical learning progress.

But, today's general music teachers are already busy enough teaching hundreds of students. Aren't music assessments "more demands on our time?" Not really, *if* we consider that music assessments are not add-ons to the curriculum, but are instructional activities used like tools to measure student learning during regular music lessons. *We don't stop teaching music,* and our *students don't stop making music.* Music assessment is not separate from instruction; it *is* instructional.

It would be misleading to say there isn't additional record-keeping or paperwork for the general music teacher who conducts music assessments. Being organized helps! But, in many general music situations (500-700 students is an *average* full-time load), assessment is more a matter of creative time management than increased work demands. It's like reallocating the minutes we already use—a "time trade-off." The minutes we waste with off-task, unrelated learning experiences or discipline problems that occur with unfocused students are replaced with valuable minutes spent teaching effectively to the assessment. The end result: *more efficient music teaching and learning occur in less time.*

So, let's sum up. It makes good educational sense for the general music teacher to assess musical learning in order to:

♫ ...music assessment is more a matter of creative time management than increased work demands.

- provide evidence of musical learning for evaluation and report card grades
- focus teaching and learning toward specific music content standards or learner objectives
- provide accountability for general music as a core, academic course of study
- adapt or refine musical instruction
- give feedback to both teacher and student

Note: For the overburdened music teacher who, for example, teaches 1000 students weekly, or is allowed only 20 minutes instructional time weekly per class, or serves several schools weekly, it is impossible to conduct music assessments effectively. Under these conditions, it is likewise impossible to *teach* music effectively, or for that matter, any other subject. School districts that force these kinds of unfavorable conditions on music teachers need to reconsider their commitment to *quality* music education for their students—Is the general music program offering in-depth musical instruction with reinforcement over time, or is the music program merely "warehousing" students?

SSESSMENT AS INSTRUCTION – THE *NEW* WAY

Assessment drives instruction. This means we must teach what we need to assess. With many levels of music students and learner objectives, how do general music teachers decide *what* should be assessed? The voluntary *Nine National Standards* with related achievement standards are one place to begin. (See p. 34.) The *Performance Standards for Music* are another (See Resources, p. 42). And music standards or learner objectives from local music curricula are other resources. In most school districts, it is ultimately up to the individual music teacher to decide which units are taught and when, the method of instruction, and the ways of assessing, documenting and evaluating student musical learning progress.

It's sensible to classify music assessment beneath large, "umbrella concepts" or elements of music, such as: rhythm, melody, form, tone color, meter, harmony, style, music history and appreciation, and connect that learning to specific music standards or objectives. (For the purposes of this kit, we will classify music assessment beneath the large concept *rhythm,* and connect it to Music Content Standard #4 - Composing Music and Music Standard #5 - Reading and Notating Music).

Beneath an umbrella concept, many sub concepts or elements of music are also taught, but lack of time prevents the general music teacher from assessing everything that is taught. For example, during a rhythm unit, students might also be engaged in learning beat, tempo and dynamics. But in the end, the assessment activity classifies student learning beneath one large concept—*rhythm.*

It's sensible to classify music assessment beneath large, "umbrella concepts" or elements of music...

So, what musical learning should be assessed? Addressing these questions will help: Will the newly acquired skills, knowledge, attitudes and beliefs attained by my students from this unit of instruction enable them to move forward and learn at other levels of the music curriculum? Will this musical learning encourage my students to become life-long musical learners and educated consumers of music? If the answers are "yes," then it's probably a good choice. As educational trends move away from coverage of lots of material to in-depth learning of smaller, but more meaningful chunks, the result is increased personal understanding and greater learning value. Today, the choices general music teachers make about *what to teach and assess* are more important than ever.

What Is Authentic Assessment?

The term *authentic assessment* refers to any kind of activity whereby a student demonstrates a meaningful understand of, or ability to apply, learned skills and knowledge in a real world context. It is the ultimate indicator of internalized, competent learning. For example, if a music assessment measures a student's ability to read and perform pitches B-A-G on the soprano recorder, an authentic assessment would require the student to demonstrate reading and performing music with those pitches on a soprano recorder. Assessment would not be considered authentic if the student were required to take a written test about reading and playing the recorder.

The above scenario describes an authentic assessment of a learned musical *skill*—reading and performing music on the soprano recorder. But what about measuring the development of musical *knowledge?* For example, students have been learning about different kinds of musical form – AB, ABA, Rondo (ABACADA), Theme and Variations, etc. The general music teacher might decide on two different kinds of music assessment to measure the development of musical knowledge:

1) a **listening assessment,** whereby students listen to unfamiliar samples of AB, ABA, or Rondo form, and apply learned knowledge to those samples by correctly identifying each form
2) a **project assessment,** whereby cooperative-learning groups demonstrate their knowledge of Theme and Variations by composing a group musical theme, with individuals composing variations on that theme - melody, rhythm, meter, timbre, etc.; and sharing their performance for peer assessment.

Sometimes, the use of several different kinds of assessments (both quantitative and qualitative) that measure learning is collectively referred to as *authentic assessment,* because the summation of all assessment processes and data shows evidence of meaningful, musical learning in a real world context over time.

♫ Planning backward is the key to designing a meaningful music assessment.

Quantitative Assessment refers to the analysis of learning evidence from concrete, objective products. Quantitative assessment uses points, scales, ratings, percentages, charts, graphs, sub-totals and totals.

Qualitative Assessment refers to the analysis of learning evidence from subjective, less concrete processes. Qualitative assessment uses observations, reflections, interviews, opinions, surveys and questionnaires.

How To Design and Integrate Music Assessment

How do we design a meaningful music assessment? Planning backward is key. We predict specifically *what our students should know and be able to demonstrate* by the end of the unit; then we prescribe *what they need to learn* in order to do that. For example, at the beginning of a rhythm unit, we explain to students that at the end of the unit we will measure their competency at performing and notating certain rhythm patterns. We describe task criteria that they are expected to meet or exceed.

From the start, students are aware that they are responsible for their own learning, and that they will be expected to demonstrate that. (Students tell us they are more motivated to accept learning challenges when *they* know what to expect.) We music teachers become extremely picky in our choices of learning activities, because they all must teach to the assessment. Throughout the unit, the music teacher acts as lesson facilitator, consultant and cheerleader, while students strive to acquire the skills and knowledge to be assessed.

Integrating music assessment into our teaching style is a new thing for many of us. And, like any other new thing, it is learned gradually. Evolution, not revolution! We build our music assessment tool kit *one tool at a time with one grade level at a time.* It is recommended that we start with one upper elementary level, ex. grade 4. Then, next year we continue with the same student group in grade 5, while adding another grade level, and so on. Most of all, we must be very patient with ourselves as we progress through change.

USIC ASSESSMENT PAGE

By and large, many of the music assessment page models studied for this project were too lengthy or too complicated for use with hundreds of students in the general music classroom. A music assessment page for general music must convey learning information that is thorough yet brief. It must be simple and easy to read. And, a music assessment page should include curricular language worded for the student to understand. The above criteria necessitated the development of the Music Assessment Page in this kit.

It is recommended that the Music Assessment Page be used for Grades 3+. Although not impossible, it may be unrealistic to expect K-2 students to comprehend an assessment page. Confusion impedes learning. For younger students, general music teachers may simply elect to describe the learning expectations at the beginning of a unit, and conduct a music assessment at the end of the unit. Of course, the Music Assessment Page can be adapted and used for reporting and communicating assessment information for any grade level as needed.

Please note Sample Music Assessment Page on p. 10. After you have created your own Music Assessment Page master from the template on p. 35, use colored paper if possible when reproducing it for student use. Colored Music Assessment Pages are easily differentiated from other music pages, songs, assignments, etc.

A music assessment page for general music must convey learning information that is thorough yet brief.

Concept

The *Concept* is the large umbrella concept or element of music beneath which the assessed skills or knowledge can be classified. On your Music Assessment Page master, write the concept on the blank line.

Music Standard or Learner Objective

The *Music Standard* or *Learner Objective* is the specific learned skill or knowledge being assessed. Perhaps you have designed your music assessment to meet one or more of the Nine National Standards for Music Education (music content standard or achievement standard), or one or more of the Performance Standards for Music; or one or more learner objectives from your school district's music curriculum. On your Music Assessment Page master, write the standard(s) or learner objective(s) on the blank line.

Icon

The *Icon* is a graphic that illustrates the music assessment. Although not essential, it does give visual learners a helpful "snapshot" of what is being assessed. Reproducible graphics can be obtained through "clip art" books, or computer software. Reproduce appropriate graphic, cut out and paste on upper right blank portion of your Music Assessment Page master.

Sample

MUSIC ASSESSMENT PAGE

Date: 10/19/99
Grading Period: Sem. 1

Name: Michael Cummings   Music Teacher: Mrs. Lavender
Class: 5-©AL

GRADE 5

MUSIC ASSESEMENT # 1

Concept: Rhythm

Music Standard or Learner Objective: Music Standard #4 - Composing Music #5 - Reading and Notating Music

A TASK (check √)

Self Assessor(s): Mrs. Lavender Tawny R.

- ☑ ☑ 1-Compose one measure of rhythm in meter of 4.
- ☐ ☐ 2-Perform eight measures of rhythm with few or no mistakes.
- ☑ ☑ 3-Notate rhythms from memory with minimum of six correct measures.

*If student is unable to participate with appropriate musical team behavior, assessment score is lowered one point.

B ASSESSMENT

At this time the learner...

- ☐ **3+** exceeds
- ☐ **3** consistently demonstrates
- ☑ **2** is developing
- ☐ **1** is beginning to develop
- ☐ **0** is unable to demonstrate

...competency at the task with meaningful, musical understanding.

Nice effort, Mike!
Let's keep working on half notes 𝅗𝅥 = 2 beats and dotted half notes 𝅗𝅥. = 3 beats

C REFLECTION

Please explain the difference between the beat and rhythm of music.

The beat just stays the same and the rhythm goes long or short like the words to the song.

Task and Rubric

The *Task* is the work a student does to demonstrate competency of learned skills or knowledge. The assessment task can be one job, or several jobs that are all part of one task. Competency at the task is determined by task criteria, called the rubric (see below). Three is a reasonable number of task points (criteria) that can be used by one general music teacher with many students. On the Sample Music Assessment Page on p. 10, Section A shows the assessment task.

A *rubric* (task criteria) is the set of scoring guidelines used to measure competency of a student's demonstration of learned skills or knowledge. The rubric answers the question: What does competency or varying degrees of competency at this task look like?

There are two kinds of rubrics:

1. *additive rubric* - lists the various elements of the task being assessed (as separate jobs) in a non-sequential manner as separate task points; earning any task point is not dependent on earning any other task point; earning all task points indicates competency or beyond (exceeds competency).
2. *continuous rubric* - lists in sequence the varying degrees of competency demonstrated at the task being assessed (one job); attainment of any degree of competency depends on the attainment of all previous degrees; earning the highest degree indicates competency or beyond (exceeds competency).

Use demonstration verbs that elicit specific behaviors.

Let's analyze the kind of task rubric used on the Sample Music Assessment Page, p. 10. Note the use of *demonstration verbs* that elicit specific behaviors. In Section A, the three task points are:

1–*Compose* one measure of rhythm in meter of 4.

2–*Perform* eight measures of rhythm with few or no mistakes.

3–*Notate* rhythms from memory with minimum of six correct measures.

This particular task rubric uses an *additive rubric.* It lists the three task points (three jobs) being assessed, none of which is dependent upon the attainment of another. Successful completion of all three task points indicates competency at the task.

Now, let's see what the task points might look like if this rhythm assessment used a *continuous rubric* with varying degrees of competency to assess the demonstration of learned rhythms (one job):

3–*Performs* eight measures of rhythm with steady beat and 0-2 mistakes.

2–*Performs* eight measures of rhythm with steady beat and 3-4 mistakes.

1–*Performs* eight measures of rhythm with mostly inaccurate rhythms and inconsistent beat.

On the Sample Music Assessment Page, p.10, notice that musicians' manners are built right into the assessment with a statement located beneath the Task in Section A: *If student is unable to participate with appropriate musical team behavior, assessment score is lowered one point.* In a real world musical setting, manners are an expectation of any successful musical organization. For example, members are expected to follow a conductor's directions; play and cut-off at appropriate times; and treat one another and instruments with respect. And so, to be a valid assessment, that same real world behavior expectation can be built into the music assessment.

On your Music Assessment Page master, in Section A, write three task points *(continuous rubric* or *additive rubric)* on the blank lines. Number the task points 1-2-3 for an *additive rubric,* or 3-2-1 for a *continuous rubric.* Try to keep the wording as consistent as possible with demonstration verbs that elicit specific behaviors, such as:

chant, clap, compose, conduct, count, create, dance, dramatize, draw, identify, list, listen, match, memorize, move, notate, observe, play, perform, read, show, sing, speak, start/stop, write, etc.

During the actual assessment activity, the assessor's name(s) is written in Section A on the blank line. The assessor can be the teacher or self only; teacher and self; peer and self; or teacher, peer and self.

...musicians' manners are built right into the assessment.

Assessment

The *Assessment* is an analysis of competency with which a student demonstrates learned skills or knowledge. In Section B of the Sample Music Assessment Page, p. 10, the degree of competency demonstrated at the task is expressed as an *assessment statement*:

"At this time, the learner ...

- ❑ **3+** *exceeds*
- ❑ **3** *consistently demonstrates*
- ❑ **2** *is developing*
- ❑ **1** *is beginning to develop*
- ❑ **0** *is unable to demonstrate*

...competency at the task with meaningful, musical understanding.

Reflection

The *Reflection* is the final, most important step in authentic music assessment. In the Reflection, the student reveals a personal, meaningful understanding of learned skills or knowledge (internalization), plus feelings, attitudes and beliefs about the learning. On your Music Assessment Page master, in Section C, construct a Reflection question or problem, using demonstration verbs that evoke a thought process. Here are some demonstration verbs sequenced according to Bloom's taxonomy. (In the 1950's Benjamin Bloom, an educational psychologist, classified the complexity of human thought into six levels known as "Bloom's Taxonomy.") Levels of thought range from simple knowledge/recall of information to higher-level reasoning:

1. **Knowledge:** *define, describe, find, identify, label, locate, recognize, select, tell*
2. **Comprehension:** *define, describe, explain, illustrate, match, summarize*
3. **Application:** *adapt, compute, discover, gather, prepare, revise, show, solve, survey, use*
4. **Analysis:** *categorize, classify, compare, contrast, predict, relate*
5. **Synthesis:** *combine, compose, create, design, develop, invent, make, organize, produce*
6. **Evaluation:** *critique, decide, evaluate, judge, justify, recommend*

In the Reflection, the student reveals a personal, meaningful understanding of learned skills or knowledge...

Sample Reflection questions or problems:

- Illustrate the kind of harmony used in canon with a simple drawing.
- How is an Egyptian lute the same as a guitar? How is it different?
- Explain why covering more holes on the soprano recorder makes the pitch sound lower.
- What is the difference between beat and rhythm?
- Decide which part of the concert was the most musically interesting to you. Please explain with at least one musical reason.
- If you had to define music to an alien, what would you say?
- Describe what worked well in your musical composition. Describe what could be improved.
- Identify at least two characteristics that make your favorite melody interesting.
- Predict what music will sound like in the year 2050.
- Classify these songs into musical styles: Twinkle Twinkle Little Star, Star Spangled Banner, Rock Around The Clock, Oh When The Saints Go Marching In, Consider Yourself - *spiritual, folk song, Broadway, rock and roll, patriotic.*

Sample LESSON PLAN FOR MUSIC ASSESSMENT
"RHYTHM RALLY" (Grade 5)

Please remember that with this music assessment activity, students are engaged as with any other classroom music activity, except it is designed as a measuring tool so the teacher can *observe* and *record learning data* throughout the lesson.

Preparation:

1. Reproduce seating chart, and insert in a clear, plastic page protector. Obtain a transparency marker.
2. Reproduce Music Assessment Page (p. 35), one copy per student on colored paper (front shows assessment information; back shows RHYTHM RALLY blank measures with beat clues – see sample on p. 15).
3. Obtain one sheet of blank paper and pencil for each student.
4. Obtain large wipe-away chart, or use chalkboard.

Remember *if* the teacher has wisely selected teaching strategies and learning activities that teach to the assessment, most students will be able to perform with competence.

Presentation:

1. Students are seated according to seating chart. *Record student absences in grade book now; eliminates confusion later.
2. Describe three task points on Music Assessment Page.
3. Instruct students to compose one rhythm pattern (using previously learned notes and rests) to equal a measure in meter of 4.
4. Check notations for accuracy. On seating chart, jot down task point number next to students' names who are unable to demonstrate that point with a brief comment for improvement. For example, *Carolyn Thompson–#1 notes/rests must equal 4 beats per measure.*
5. Collect papers, and flip like flash cards as students clap and chant the rhythm patterns as a review. (A recording of music with strong beat, such as a march, can be played as an accompaniment.)
6. Select any eight pages and copy on wipe-away chart or chalkboard or attatch pages to a magnetic surface. Title this piece RHYTHM RALLY. (See p. 15).
7. Conduct students through a clapped performance of all eight measures of RHYTHM RALLY.
8. Choose any student to erase or remove one measure. Conduct all eight measures again, including blank measure. Observe students in small groups at a time, checking for rhythmic accuracy. (Even with peer support, it becomes obvious if a student is able or unable to perform learned rhythm patterns accurately. Remember, *if* the teacher has wisely selected teaching strategies and learning activities that teach to the assessment, most students will be able to perform the rhythm patterns with competence. Few students will be unable to demonstrate competency.)
9. Another student erases or removes a second measure. Conduct the clapped performance again, including two blank measures. Continue to observe, and on seating chart, jot down task point number next to students' names who are unable to demonstrate that point with a *brief* comment for improvement. For example, *Michael Cummings - #2 hold half note for two beats and dotted half note for three beats.*

10. Continue in same manner until every measure of RHYTHM RALLY is erased.
11. While students view eight blank measures, conduct the final round. At this point, students perform the rhythm patterns entirely from memory.
12. Immediately distribute Music Assessment Pages and pencils. Invite students to notate a minimum of six correct measures over the heartbeat clues.
13. Students self-assess Part A on the front of Music Assessment Page, and respond to the Reflection in Part C (see Sample Music Assessment Page, pg. 10). The Reflection requires a *brief,* honest response to a question or problem which enables them to reveal a personal, meaningful understanding (internalization) of learned skills or knowledge.
14. Peer assess for notation accuracy by exchanging papers and showing the eight original rhythm measures. Peer writes name on Assessor blank line in Part A.

The Music Assessment Page is a tangible and valuable piece of learning evidence that shows the student's learning strengths and areas for improvement.

Note: As with K-2 students, music assessment for Grades 3+ does not automatically imply use of the Music Assessment Page. When lack of time and/or class overload prevent its use, the results of a music assessment may be simply recorded right into the Teacher Grade Book during the lesson. Remember though, that students won't have the same advantage as the teacher of seeing their learning progress recorded on paper. The Music Assessment Page is a tangible and valuable piece of learning evidence that shows the student learning strengths and areas for improvement. *It is a learning receipt.*

*In the event of student absences, general music teachers have a few options. One is to not make up the assessment, and average all other assessment points when calculating the report card grade. Another option is to schedule a make-up assessment during the next music lesson with remaining students engaged in a separate activity. A third option, if at all possible, is to schedule a make-up during recess.

RHYTHM RALLY

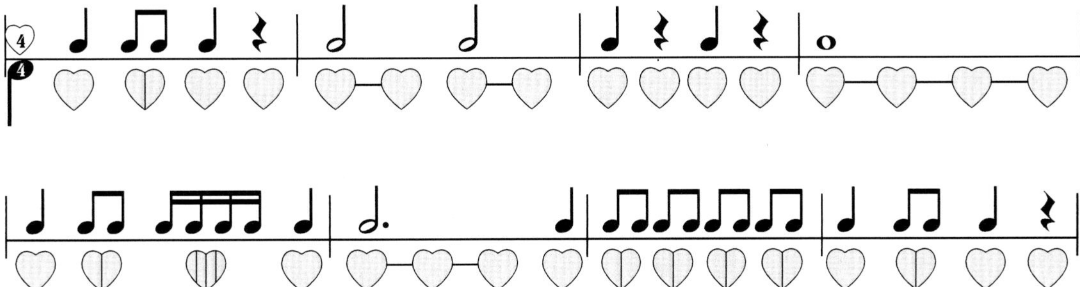

RECORDING ASSESSMENT POINTS

Please note Sample Music Assessment Page, p. 10. In Section A, the two marked boxes show two earned *additive rubric* task points. (If this assessment had used a *continuous rubric,* marking only the second box - "2" would show two earned task points - the second task point plus the "assumed" first point beneath it).

Collect student Music Assessment Pages. Select the pages of students who were unable to earn all three task points. In Section A, mark earned task points with a quick check mark; in Section B, mark box showing total number of earned task points.

On remaining students' Music Assessment Pages (those with three earned task points) in Section A, quickly mark all three task points; in Section B, quickly mark the box showing three total earned task points.

Note: If a student demonstrates exceptional skill or knowledge such that s/he *exceeds* competency at the task, it is important to mark this box (3+) in Section B with a brief comment regarding the special achievement. For example, *Grace Butcher: Wow! You composed some fun and complicated rhythms beyond those we learned in class! Bravo!*

Next, take out your Teacher Grade Book, and *first* mark those students who were unable to earn three task points with the number of points they did earn; next, mark those who earned 3+ points; then, go quickly down class list and mark three points for remaining students. (Remember, you already marked absent students.)

This grade book process takes about seven to ten minutes for an average class of 25 students.

Done!

This grade book process takes about seven to ten minutes for an *average* class of 25 students. (The clear, plastic page protector covering the seating chart can be wiped off and reused with future assessments; or the written data can be reproduced and filed; or data can be recorded in a different color for each assessment, accumulating on plastic covered seating charts throughout the grading period.)

Music Assessment Pages can be stored in student music portfolios (see Student Music Portfolios, p. 33), or sent home.

Aman, Mohammed	3	2		3			Ab(3)			3		1	3	song	18	A
Butcher, Grace	3	2		3+	2		2	2		3			3	piano sonatina	20+	A+
Carson, Abraham	3			3			3			2			1	"Stage Hand"	12	B
Crawford, Brett	3			3			1			2			3	homemade instrument & comp.	12	B
Cummings, Michael	**2**	**2**		**3**			**3**	**2**		**3**			**3**	**trumpet-Fanfare**	**18**	**A**
Donnelly, Cassandra	3			2			3			3		1	3	harmonica-Skip to My Lou	15	A-
Drewa, Ashka	3			2			3			3			3	dance-jazz	14	B+
Epstein, Isha	3			3			3			3			1	"M.C."	13	B+
Jackson, LaQuita	3+	2		3	2		3	2		3		1	3	dance trio-rap	22+	A+
Larsen, Jennifer	1	2		3			3			3			3	dance trio-rap	15	A-
Murphy, Jason	3	2		3	2		3			3			3	violin duet-Gavotte	19	A
	3			Ab(2)			2			1			1	"Checker"	9	C+
														"Award Presenter"	12	B

ASSESSMENT STRATEGIES

There are as many ways to assess musical learning as there are general music teachers. Assessment strategies can be learned by attending clinics and seminars; reading music education journals; and networking with other general music teachers who conduct successful music assessments in similar music programs. Over time you will acquire a collection of assessment strategies that will work time and again in your unique general music program.

Gaining in popularity is the use of an electronic, hand-held device known as a PDA (personal digital assistant). Like the Palm Pilot (manufactured by Palm Computing, Inc), this device allows the teacher to roam the music room, documenting student learning as it happens. Some PDAs have a docking station that allows users to transfer information between the PDA and a desktop computer. If you store assessment data and grades on a desktop computer, consider the time-saving and organizational advantages of a PDA.

Informal Assessment Strategies

Informal Assessment Strategies are activities conducted by the teacher who needs immediate feedback on the learning level of the class. (With some informal strategies, students may be unaware that they are even being assessed.) With this feedback, the teacher can adapt or refine instruction. Following are some examples:

Informal Assessment Strategies are activities conducted by the teacher who needs immediate feedback on the learning level of the class.

- For assessing the ability to **sing a song in tune,** teacher roams among students, listening and documenting intonation data on a seating chart for two consecutive lessons. Students' intonation capabilities can be seen at a glance right on the seating chart.
- For whole-group self assessment of **active listening skills,** students rate their listening efforts with a show of fingers 1-2-3-4-5; 5 indicating best effort and 1 indicating least effort.
- For assessing the ability to discern **different meters,** students listen to recorded samples of meter in 2, meter in 3, and meter in 4, and respond by holding up the appropriate number of fingers to their chests.
- For quick spot-check assessment of **timbre recognition,** while a recording is playing, teacher roams the room, and randomly invites students to whisper the names of the instrument(s) being heard in teacher's ear. Or, the same technique can be used for melody recognition, as students "whisper that tune" in teacher's ear.
- For whole-group self assessment of a **song performance,** teacher says: "Please show me how well you think our class demonstrates energetic, enthusiastic singing with our patriotic song. Thumbs *up* indicates lots of energy; thumbs *middle* indicates some energy; thumbs *down* indicates lack of energy."

Formal Assessment Strategies

Formal Assessment Strategies include activities during which students demonstrate learned skills or knowledge for the purpose of assessing, documenting and evaluating musical learning. Following are strategies that have worked well in many general music situations. Use these strategies as springboards from which to adapt or develop your own creative assessment strategies:

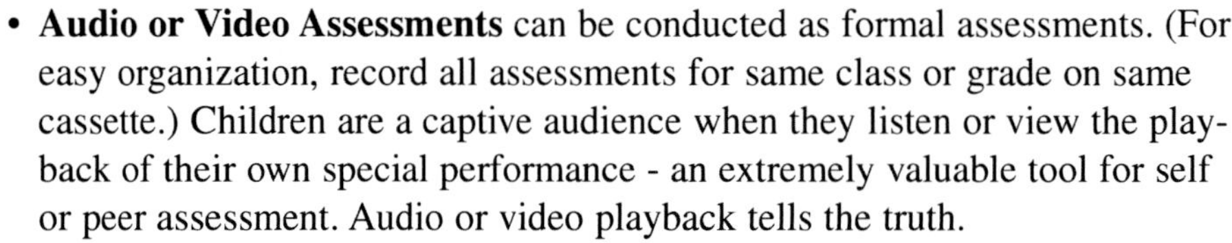

- **Audio or Video Assessments** can be conducted as formal assessments. (For easy organization, record all assessments for same class or grade on same cassette.) Children are a captive audience when they listen or view the playback of their own special performance - an extremely valuable tool for self or peer assessment. Audio or video playback tells the truth.
- For assessing performance of **steady beat** (or rhythm), teacher randomly distributes color "place mats" (construction paper), one per student - ex. blue, green, yellow, red, orange. Teacher keeps one paper of each color, plus 3 of another color (ex. purple), to use as flash cards. Teacher scrambles flash cards and sets on music stand. While music plays, first color is shown. Students with same color place mat perform steady beat (or rhythm) on their instrument while teacher observes and documents competency for this small group. Next color is shown, and a new group of performers is assessed. When the color purple is visible, all perform. Activity continues in same fashion until all flash cards have been used.

Formal Assessment Strategies...for the purpose of assessing, documenting and evaluating musical learning.

- Assessing **singing skills** (posture, breath control, intonation, enunciation, and expression, etc., can be accomplished with small groups at a time working near the teacher. For example, a small group of 5 students is labeled 1-2-3-4-5. When teacher says: "All," entire class sings together; when teacher says: "1-2" only those two students sing; when teacher says: "3," only that student sings; and so on. When teacher has documented performance data for each member of small group, another small group is assessed in the same manner. With this kind of assessment, many songs can be sung instead of one song many times.
- Colorful, stretchy wrist bands can be worn by all students being assessed during **folk dancing.** All students dance, but a designated small group of students wear bands on ankles - they are the ones being observed and documented during this portion of the dance. Part way through, stop and start again with a new assessment group wearing bands on ankles.
- For assessing **rhythmic or melodic improvisation,** teacher conducts a Rondo piece, with Part A being the theme played by all. At Part B, first four students in turn improvise 4 or 8 measures of rhythm or melody, while rest of class snaps to the beat for support. At Part A, entire class performs altogether again. At Part C, next four students improvise in turn. Activity continues in this manner until all students have improvised. During each student improvisation, teacher observes and documents learning data.

- Popsicle sticks work great for taking turns during performances of **student compositions.** Popsicle sticks are numbered on one end, one for each student, and placed numbered side down into a mug or paper cup. Students "count off" to determine own number. Teacher draws out first stick - student with matching number performs first. During performance, teacher observes and documents learning data. An adapted peer assessment page keeps remaining students engaged by requiring them to assess the same tasks. Current performer picks next popsicle stick.
- For a project assessment with **sound production,** students invent an instrument for the "tin can band." With "found" items, such as paper plates, beads, paper towel tubes, wire, tin cans, balloons, cardboard boxes, masking tape, rubber bands, lengths of pipe, clothes hangers, string, etc., students can work alone or together for homework to create a new musical instrument. In class, they can play the instrument and describe its particular sound specifications. Self and peer assessment is valuable. This assessment works well when collaborating with the science teacher.
- Students learning to **play melodies on bells or keyboards** can choose which of three melodies they want to be assessed on. Teacher distributes "tickets" to all students. Students may perform all three melodies, but the students being assessed place their ticket in front of their bells or keyboard. Teacher observes and documents learning data for these small groups at a time.

Games offer fun opportunites during music assessment with rewards.

- **Games** offer fun opportunities during music assessment with rewards. For "Music Tic Tac Toe," Teacher sets up a Tic Tac Toe grid at the board, and fills each of nine areas with a different, learned rhythm pattern that match lyrics to learned songs. Students are divided into two teams, **A** and **B**. Teacher sings and claps one rhythm. First student on Team **A** finds the correct rhythm and draws **A** near the rhythm. Teacher documents response. If incorrect, student may collaborate with others on the team until correct rhythm is found. Game continues in this fashion, until one team scores a Tic Tac Toe. Substitute rhythms from other songs, and play game as many times as necessary until each student responds three times. Teacher documents all responses.

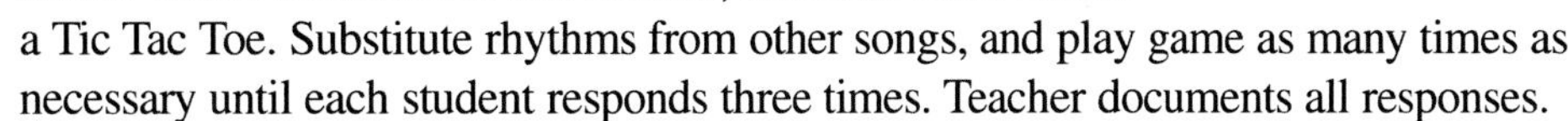

- **Journal writings** are ongoing accounts of students' own personal reflections. With journal writing, students share personal attitudes and beliefs about music and learning - evidence of meaningful, musical processing. Journal entries can include reflections about musical performance, composition, listening activities, the importance of music in their lives, influential musicians, etc.
- **Interviews, Surveys, or Questionnaires** afford students opportunities to communicate to the music teacher information about their learning styles, strengths and weaknesses. A Student Musical Profile is an interview on paper conducted at the beginning of the year. Students are invited to complete this survey of questions about their background, including past musical experiences, current music reading level, favorite music, family life, interests, hobbies, etc. For *differentiated* instruction and assessment, a Student Musical Profile reveals the learning level at which each student should be challenged.
- Formal Assessment strategies also can include traditional **tests, quizzes, assignments,** and other written student work products.

Ongoing Assessment: Team Participation

Team Participation Assessment is an ongoing assessment of student effort and participation, and should be included when calculating the music grade. Please note Sample MUSI-CARD on p. 26-27. In the Assessment column, Team Participation is the last assessment entry. Remember, we assess what we teach. Can we teach appropriate team participation? Of course we can. Here is one way:

At the beginning of the school year, students set their own guidelines for team participation. For example, classes can brainstorm guidelines for appropriate team participation. The music teacher takes the three most popular suggestions, and prints them on a classroom poster.

1. Choose to ... have a good learning attitude.

2. Choose to ... take turns.

3. Choose to ... respect people and instruments.

At the start of the grading period, all third grade students are told that they are *automatically* given three assessment points for Team Participation. Throughout the grading period, the teacher models the guidelines, and positively reinforces appropriate team participation behaviors in students who demonstrate them. With a new unit, the teacher can describe *specific* behaviors needed for learning success: "During this unit with the Orff instruments, I will need to observe students taking turns, keeping mallets safe and in control, and starting/stopping at my direction. Let me show you some examples of what I mean."

Students who consistently demonstrate appropriate behavior choices (keeping the team moving forward) throughout the grading period, keep the three Team Participation Assessment points toward their report card grade. Students who prevent the team from moving forward due to inappropriate behavior choices lose Team Participation Assessment points (ex. 2-5 participation reminders = lose 1 point; 6-10 participation reminders = lose 2 points, or whatever policy is established). In these cases, the music teacher intervenes with behavior modification techniques to guide students toward more appropriate behavior choices.

Perhaps the most compelling reason to include Team Participation Assessment as part of music assessment and the report card grade is that, as ongoing assessment, students are held accountable for their own learning behavior. With Team Participation Assessment, there is an increase in student motivation and focus, and a decrease in classroom discipline problems. Although many activities in the general music classroom are perceived to be "fun and enjoyable," it is truly gratifying to see students take their participation in music class "seriously."

With Team Participation Assessment, there is an increase in student motivation and focus, and a decrease in classroom discipline problems.

Note: All Assessments need to be *modified* for adaptive education students, or students who are placed on special "individual education plans" or other learning/behavior plans which allow for modified learner expectations and/or grades.

IOW OFTEN TO ASSESS

Because general music teachers teach hundreds of students, and are required to calculate semesterly or quarterly report card grades, it is recommended that a *maximum* of four music assessments be conducted semesterly, or two music units/assessments quarterly. The number of music assessments per grading period is flexible, so the music teacher can plan with *realistic* expectations. Consider that some music programs offer lessons daily or two-three days per week, while other programs offer lessons only once weekly or twice monthly. A comprehensive unit on jazz could take up the entire 9 weeks of one quarter! Parameters such as these dictate the number of music assessments that can be conducted in one grading period.

Remember, every unit that is taught does not have to be assessed. If you are just starting to integrate music assessment into your instruction, begin with only one or two music assessments during the entire grading period with one grade level. Following are sample music assessment schedules:

	School Year	=	**36 weeks**
	Semester	=	**18 weeks**
	#1 Music Assessment	=	9 weeks
	#2 Music Assessment	=	9 weeks
	#3 Team Participation Assessment	=	ongoing
OR			
	#1 Music Assessment	=	6 weeks
	#2 Music Assessment	=	6 weeks
	#3 Music Assessment	=	6 weeks
	#4 Team Participation Assessment	=	ongoing
OR			
	#1 Music Assessment	=	4.5 weeks
	#2 Music Assessment	=	4.5 weeks
	#3 Music Assessment	=	4.5 weeks
	#4 Music Assessment	=	4.5 weeks
	#5 Team Participation Assessment	=	ongoing
OR			
	#1 Music Assessment	=	9 weeks
	#2 Music Assessment	=	4.5 weeks
	#3 Music Assessment	=	4.5 weeks
	#4 Team Participation Assessment	=	ongoing
	Quarter	=	**9 weeks**
	#1 Music Assessment	=	9 weeks
	#2 Team Participation Assessment	=	ongoing
OR			
	#1 Music Assessment	=	6 weeks
	#2 Music Assessment	=	3 weeks
	#3 Team Participation Assessment	=	ongoing
OR			
	#1 Music Assessment	=	4.5 weeks
	#2 Music Assessment	=	4.5 weeks
	#3 Team Participation Assessment	=	ongoing

The number of music assessments per grading period is flexible, so the music teacher can plan with realistic expectations.

The next section, *EVALUATION–THE MUSIC GRADE* explores music evaluation and report card grades. If your school district does not require report card grades for communicating music evaluation, you can proceed to the section after that titled *MUSI-CARD.*

EVALUATION – THE MUSIC GRADE

The *evaluation* (judgment) reported as a music grade is calculated by adding together all assessment points, plus any other points offered during the grading period. Other points are entirely *optional,* and might include *Homework* or *Bonus* points.

For the general music teacher who can manage it, a brief but creative *Homework* page *(simple, but ya gotta think)* for students in Grades 3+, reveals musical learning in yet another way. (It may be unrealistic to assign music homework to K-2 students). One Homework page, worth for example, two homework points, can be offered with each unit, and due at the end of the unit. Music Homework pages should be short and simple, so correction is fast and easy. Be sure to include due date at top of Homework page.

Talent Day is one way to offer *Bonus* points. Each semester, Talent Day is held during regular music class (ex. two half-hour periods) as an opportunity for students to share music in a way that is personally meaningful to them. Students who prepare an act or report for Talent Day earn three Bonus points - equal to a music assessment. For example, students can sing a favorite song, perform a composed melody, create a dance to favorite music, play a homemade instrument, etc. Students in band or orchestra perform a piece of music on their instrument. Students who take private lessons perform their piano, guitar or dance solo, etc. Students can also present a report describing their favorite music, performing group, instrument, or concert, complete with visual aids.

Talent Day is one way to offer Bonus points.

General music teachers who conduct Talent Day say they are startled to discover talent and unique musical backgrounds that would otherwise remain undetected during regular music class. *(This* music teacher has had the remarkable good fortune of witnessing students perform for Talent Day on bagpipe, penny whistle, harp, dulcimer, djembe, wood flute, chord organ, harmonica, spoons, and all sorts of fascinating homemade sound makers—not the typical instrumentarium found in most general music classrooms!) Students who help during Talent Day as "stage crew" earn one Bonus point. (A guide for conducting Talent Day can be found in the Hal Leonard Classroom Resource, *It's Your Turn ... Again!* Book - #08740696 / CD - #08740892)

By offering additional Homework or Bonus points, students are allowed *other* meaningful ways of demonstrating their unique musicianship and/or personal understanding of music in the world around them. And, for students who are not always able to demonstrate competency on music assessments, Homework or Bonus points gives them other chances to "beef up" music points toward the report card grade of *their* choice.

So, back to the evaluation. At the beginning of a grading period, the general music teacher predetermines the breakdown of all possible points into the grading scale required by the school district. (Grading scales vary: ABCDF; 1-2-3; Excellent,

Satisfactory Plus, Satisfactory, Needs Improvement; + or -; even smiley or sad faces!) Following is a sample of a grading scale with *only* Assessment points (no Homework or Bonus points) for a semester grading period, using two different grading scales:

Semester	**=**	**18 weeks**	
#1 Music Assessment	=	6 weeks	(3 possible points)
#2 Music Assessment	=	6 weeks	(3 possible points)
#3 Music Assessment	=	6 weeks	(3 possible points)
#4 Team Participation Assessment	=	ongoing	(3 possible points)
			12 total possible points

Points	Grade
10-11-**12**	Excellent
7-8-9	Satisfactory Plus
4-5-6	Satisfactory
1-2-3	Needs Improvement

Points	Grade
12	A+
11	A
10	A-
9	B+
8	B
7	B-
6	C+
5	C
4	C-
3	D+
2	D
1	D-
0	F

Now, let's see what those same grading scales look like with Assessment points *plus* the addition of Homework and Bonus points.

Semester	**=**	**18 weeks**	
#1 Music Assessment	=	6 weeks	(3 possible points)
#2 Music Assessment	=	6 weeks	(3 possible points)
#3 Music Assessment	=	6 weeks	(3 possible points)
#4 Team Participation Assessment	=	ongoing	(3 possible points)
Other Points:			
#1 Homework	=		(2 possible points)
#2 Homework	=		(2 possible points)
#3 Homework	=		(2 possible points)
Bonus - Talent Day	=		(3 possible points)
			21 total possible points

Points	Grade
18-19-20-**21**	Excellent
13-14-15-16-17	Satisfactory Plus
7-8-9-10-11-12	Satisfactory
1-2-3-4-5-6	Needs Improvement

Points	Grade
21	A+
20	A
18-19	A-
16-17	B+
14-15	B
12-13	B-
10-11	C+
8-9	C
6-7	C-
4-5	D+
2-3	D
1	D-
0	F

As you determine the breakdown of all possible points into your grading scale, maintain a somewhat balanced dispersement of points throughout the grading scale. For example, with a total of 12 possible assessment points, a student who earns all three task points on each of four assessments (12 pts.) is in the highest range; two task points earned on each of four assessments (8 pts.) is in the next range; one task point earned on each of four assessments (4 pts.) is in a lower range; and zero to three task points on all combined assessments is in yet the lowest range. This contrived breakdown of points is at best only a guide, as students will not earn exactly the same number of task points on every assessment. But at least it's a starting point for thinking about how to manage the breakdown of all possible points into a grading scale.

Note: In some elementary schools, fine arts grading scales do not include D or F.

MUSI-CARD

The MUSI-CARD is like a "growth chart" on which students mark earned points during a grading period. (See Sample MUSI-CARD on p. 26-27.) The MUSI-CARD shows Assessments, Homework or Bonus activities, grading scale and grade translation. During the grading period, MUSI-CARDs are stored loose in separate class bins or boxes labeled with classroom teachers' names, or attached to the inside cover of individual student portfolios. (See Student Music Portfolios, p. 33). If used in portfolios, each new grading period's MUSI-CARD is attached at the top directly over the previous MUSI-CARD. This allows for flipping through the MUSI-CARDs in order to monitor learning progress. **It is recommended that the MUSI-CARD be introduced at second semester of Grade 3, and used in each grade thereafter.**

The MUSI-CARD puts students at the center of their own learning by enabling them to own and control their learning progress. Following each MUSI-CARD activity, students mark earned points on their MUSI-CARD grid. It only takes a few moments. Students appear eager to mark their points—it seems they like the sense of accomplishment and closure. At the end of the entire grading period, students add up all earned points, and translate the sum into a music grade according to the grading scale. Of course, the teacher does likewise in Grade Book. (If students are just learning to mark points on their own MUSI-CARDs, it is helpful to monitor the point recording process. Some students become confused with a grid, and it might take a few times to get it right.)

Sometime during the start of the school year, students are instructed to fill in the upper portion of the MUSI-CARD, including name and class. (It's extremely helpful for students, especially those who happen to have special learning challenges, to watch the music teacher model these steps with a transparency of the MUSI-CARD on an overhead projector.)

The MUSI-CARD puts students at the center of their own learning by enabling them to own and control their learning progress.

Learning Goal

As an *optional* MUSI-CARD activity, students are encouraged to write a personal **Learning Goal** for music class. It is helpful to display a "bank" of learning goals, previously identified as meaningful by other music students:

Learning Goals:

- to understand more about music
- to learn about different kinds of music
- to learn how to perform music
- to become a better listener
- to become more creative
- to enjoy music more
- to become part of a music team
- other:

Sample
MUSI-CARD
Semester

GRADE *5*

MUSI-CARD

Date: *9/7/99*
Grading Period: *Sem. 1*

Name: *Michael Cummings* Music Teacher: *Mrs. Lavender*
Class: *5-ⓒAL*

Learning Goal: *to be more creative*

PRE-GRADE SELF ASSESSMENT

1. My learning strengths: *I listen well.*
2. My learning weaknesses: *Sometimes I'm not organized.*
3. Grade I desire: *A*
4. Grade I predict: *B+*

	Consistently Demonstrates or Exceeds (+) 3 pts.	Developing 2 pts.	Beginning to Develop 1 pt.	Unable to Demonstrate 0 pts.
ASSESSMENT				
1. Rhythm (Notation) - 3 pts.		2		
2. Melody (Composition) - 3 pts.	3			
3. Harmony (Guitars) - 3 pts.	3+			
4. Team Participation - 3 pts.	3			
HOMEWORK				
1. Rhythm - 2 pts.		2		
2. Melody - 2 pts.				
3. Harmony - 2 pts.		2		
BONUS				
Talent Day Act or Report - 3 pts.	3			
or Talent Day Crew - 1 pt.				
Music News Article - 1 pt.				
Sub Totals	12+	6		

Total 18+ = **Grade** A

A	Excellent
B	Above Average
C	Average
D	Below Average
F	Failure

Points	Grade
	A+
21-22	A
18-19-20	A-
15-16-17	B+
13-14	B
12	B-
10-11	C+
9	C
8	C-
6-7	D+
4-5	D
2-3	D-
1	F
0	

POST-GRADE SELF ASSESSMENT

1. How do I feel about the music grade I earned? (O.K.) or NOT O.K.
2. How can I improve my musical learning? *Keep doing my best*
3. Did I reach my Learning Goal? (YES) or NO (please explain)

When I composed my melody piece it sounded great. It was fun to write my own music.

Sample
MUSI-CARD
Quarter

GRADE 3

MUSI-CARD

Name: Shauna Williams

Class: 3-C@L Music Teacher: Mrs. Lavender Date: 3/13/00

Grading Period: 2tr. 3

1 Outstanding
2 Satisfactory
3 Needs Improvement

	Consistently Demonstrates or Exceeds (+)	Developing	Beginning to Develop	Unable to Demonstrate
ASSESSMENT	3 pts.	2 pts.	1 pt.	0 pts.
1. Melody (Recorders) - 3 pts.		2		
2. Instrument Families - 3 pts.		2		
3. Team Participation - 3 pts.	3			
BONUS				
Music In My Life Reflection - 1 pt.			1	
Sub Totals	3	4	1	

Total: 8 = Grade: 1

Points	Grade
8-9-10	1
5-6-7	2
1-2-3-4	3

Pre-Grade Self Assessment

The PRE-GRADE SELF-ASSESSMENT is another *optional* MUSI-CARD activity. Students identify their learning strengths, learning weaknesses, desired grade and predicted grade. This information is valuable for determining students' learning readiness, while enabling them to share current beliefs and attitudes about learning and music in general.

1. **My learning strengths** and 2. **My learning weaknesses.** It can be explained that successful learners consistently utilize their learning strengths while trying to improve areas of weakness. Students are invited to reflect on and identify their present learning strengths and weaknesses. Again, it is helpful for students to view a "bank" of choices:

Learning Strengths:	**Learning Weaknesses:**
• I listen well.	• Sometimes I forget to listen.
• I pay attention.	• Sometimes I can't pay attention.
• I am a leader.	• Sometimes I can't get started.
• I am a fair team player.	• Sometimes I forget to play fair.
• I try my best.	• Sometimes I don't feel like trying.
• I am patient with myself.	• Sometimes I am too hard on myself.
• I am organized.	• Sometimes I am disorganized.
• I don't give up.	• Sometimes I give up.
• I follow directions.	• Sometimes I forget to follow directions.
• I participate.	• Sometimes I don't participate.
• I cooperate.	• Sometimes I don't cooperate.
• I take turns.	• Sometimes I forget to take turns.
• I show respect.	• Sometimes I forget to show respect.
• other:	• other:

Students are invited to reflect on and identify their present learning strengths and weaknesses.

3. **Grade I desire.** Students identify the music grade that "in their wildest dreams" they would love to see on their report card. This information is an indicator of students' present level of self-esteem—necessary for learning success.

4. **Grade I predict.** Students reflect on their own learning strengths and weaknesses, and predict a music grade *slightly lower* than the grade they perceive to be realistically achievable. For example, if a student thinks that a grade of A is achievable, s/he might write A- or B+, thereby allowing some flexibility in meeting or exceeding their own prediction.

Grading Scale and Grade Translation

The Grading Scale shows the points equal to a music grade. At the beginning of the grading period, the music teacher predetermines the grading scale. The grade translation shows the meaning of each grade.

Post-Grade Self Assessment

The POST-GRADE SELF ASSESSMENT is another *optional* MUSI-CARD activity. It brings closure to the grading period by allowing students to acknowledge their feelings about the music grade they earned; identify ways to improve their musical learning; and share reflections on meeting their Learning Goal. On the next grading period's MUSI-CARD, students are encouraged to predict the *same grade or higher* as the grade they earned on the last MUSI-CARD. Most students, encouraged by their own learning success, maintain or improve their music grade with each successive MUSI-CARD.

Assembling the MUSI-CARD

1. Please note MUSI-CARD *template* on p. 36 and *cut outs* on p. 37-41.
2. To assemble the MUSI-CARD, reproduce MUSI-CARD template.
3. If desired, reproduce, cut out and paste Learning Goal and PRE-GRADE SELF ASSESSMENT near top of reproduced template. (*Cut out* on p. 37)
4. Reproduce, cut and paste ASSESSMENT grid plus HOMEWORK and/or BONUS grids (p. 38-41) as needed, on reproduced template. Next, reproduce, cut out and paste grading scale and grade translation on reproduced template. (p. 38)
5. If desired, reproduce, cut out and paste POST-GRADE SELF ASSESSMENT (p. 37) near bottom of reproduced template.
6. Reproduce the assembled MUSI-CARD. You now have a working MUSI-CARD template to use for each grading period.
7. Reproduce this working MUSI-CARD template for the grading period you are presently teaching.
8. Fill in date, music teacher name and grading period information.
9. If you already know the units you plan to assess, fill them in at this time in the ASSESSMENT column in the same numbered sequence you plan to teach them. If you do not already know the units you plan to assess, leave blank, and your students can fill in that information when they record their assessment points.
10. If you already know the Homework or Bonus activities you plan to offer, fill them in at this time in the HOMEWORK or BONUS columns in the same numbered sequence you plan to offer them. If you do not already know the Homework or Bonus activities you plan to offer, leave blank, and your students can fill in that information when they record their Homework or Bonus points.
11. You now have a MUSI-CARD master to reproduce for student use during the present grading period.

Most students, encouraged by their own learning success, maintain or improve their music grade with each successive MUSI-CARD.

Note: For the general music teacher whose school district does not require report card grades, the MUSI-CARD can be used as a communication tool for reporting student progress. Simply assemble the MUSI-CARD as desired, but eliminate the sub-totals, total, grading scale and grade translation.

TEACHER GRADE BOOK

Maintaining an organized *Teacher Grade Book* is fundamental to efficient music assessment and evaluation. Most Grade Books have a common format: class list on left page, and grids on left page extending across spine to right page. Consider using left page grids only for recording *learning data*: Assessment points, Homework points, Bonus points, point totals and report card grade. Use right page grids only for recording *other data* such as student absences, team participation reminders, behavior checks, notes, etc.

This system makes points and other grading data on left page available at a glance, without having to scan across both left and right pages. It also makes the recording of data on a single page less prone to error. Allow enough pages per class per grading period for recording data throughout the entire year. Plastic tabs (the kind used on dividers in 3-ring notebooks) labeled with classroom teachers' names, attached directly to each class page, are great for flipping quickly to the desired class. Tear out remaining unusable pages from grade book. Attach MUSI-CARDs for each grade level on inside front cover for easy reference of Assessment, Homework or Bonus activities.

Sample Semester Grade Book Page – Grade 5

Name	1. Assess Rhythm (Notation)-3 pts.	1. Homework Rhythm-2 pts.	2. Assess Melody (Composition)-3 pts.	2. Homework Melody-2 pts.	3. Assess Harmony (Guitars)-3 pts.	3. Homework Harmony-2 pts.	4. Assess Team Participation-3 pts.	Bonus Music News Article-1 pt.	Talent Day 11/15/19 (Act or Report - 3 pts. / "Stage Crew" - 1 pt.)		Total Semester Points	Semester Music Grade
Aman, Mohammed	3	2	3		Ab(3)		3	1	3	song	18	A
Butcher, Grace	3	2	3+	2	2	2	3		3	piano sonatina	20+	A+
Carson, Abraham	3		3		3		2		1	"Stage Hand"	12	B
Crawford, Brett	3		3		1		2		3	homemade instrument & comp.	12	B
Cummings, Michael	**2**	**2**	**3**		**3**	**2**	**3**		**3**	**trumpet-fanfare**	**18**	**A**
Donnelly, Cassandra	3		2		3		3	1	3	harmonica-Skip to My Lou	15	A-
Drewa, Ashka	3		2		3		3		3	dance-jazz	14	B+
Epstein, Isha	3		3		3		3		1	"M.C."	13	B+
Jackson, LaQuita	3+	2	3	2	3	2	3	1	3	dance trio-rap	22+	A+
Larsen, Jennifer	1	2	3		3		3		3	dance trio-rap	15	A-
Murphy, Jason	3	2	3	2	3		3		3	violin duet-Gavotte	19	A
O'Neal, Billy	3		Ab(2)		2		1		1	"Checker"	9	C+
Rodriquez, Tawny	3	2	3		2		1		1	"Awards Presenter"	12	B
Schutz, Wolfgang	3		3		3		3		1	"Stage Hand"	13	B+
Thompson, Carolyn	2	2	3+	2	3	2	3	1	3	dance trio-rap	21+	A+
Yang, Kim	3		3		3		3		3	violin duet-Gavotte	15	A-

STUDENT MUSIC PORTFOLIOS

A student *music portfolio* is a purposeful collection of student work that exhibits to the student and others evidence of musical development over time. The concept of portfolios for music assessment was initiated through ArtsPROPEL, a collaborative project with Howard Gardner (co-director of Harvard University's Project Zero,) the Educational Testing Service, and Boston/Pittsburgh Public Schools in the mid 1980's. (Incidentally, PROPEL is an acronym for three separate words: *pro*duction, or making music; *per*ception, listening to music; and *re*flection, thinking about and describing music.) Portfolios can take many forms: a traditional folder of papers; audio tapes; video tapes; or works saved on computer disk.

For the general music class, a traditional folder - a *process/product* portfolio, is suggested. Not unlike a scrapbook, this folder stores a student's work documents including both learning processes and finished products. This accumulation of documents over time enables students to gradually develop an ongoing assessment of their own musical development. And, the general music teacher gleans valuable information about students' learning progress, effort, work habits and more. Music portfolios are a "win-win."

During the grading period, music portfolios are stored in separate class bins or boxes labeled with classroom teachers' names. At the end of the school year, portfolios may be sent home with students. Or, in some school districts, selected pieces of students' best works from all curricular areas (including a favorite music composition or activity) are entered into a "passport portfolio." Passport portfolios advance with students from grade to grade, and are stored by the current classroom teacher.

Music portfolios are a "win-win."

Music portfolio contents can include:

- MUSI-CARDs (Grades 3+), Assessment Pages (Grades 3+), music pages, practice pages, assignments, compositions, notes, tests, quizzes, certificates of achievement, etc.
- teacher observations and comments
- student personal reflections
- journal writings
- interviews, surveys or questionnaires

Portfolios offer:

- an ongoing student musical learning profile
- student-centered learning
- opportunity for student goal-setting, assessment, reflection, documentation, and celebration of achievement
- capability for teacher and student to monitor learning progress together
- shared accountability for teacher and student in meeting music standards or learner objectives
- feedback for adapting or refining instruction
- hands-on evidence of student learning for parent/teacher conferences

A variety of card-stock folders are available at office supply stores for use as music portfolios. Since they need to last the school year, folders must be sturdy. Three-way cut letter-size manila folders work well, with student names labeled on the tabs. Pocket folders can also be used. (Folders come in colors, so grade level portfolios can be color-coded. Or, color-coded labels accomplish the same thing. Music teachers have also used large, laminated pieces of construction paper, folded in half for portfolios.

Portfolio Preparation

1. Ahead of time, label each portfolio with student name and class. (For efficiency, print out names on self-adhesive labels from master class lists stored in computer database.)
2. If the MUSI-CARD is used (Grades 3+), trim 3/8" from right or left edge with paper cutter, and attach to inside front cover; for subsequent grading periods attach new MUSI-CARD at the top directly over previous MUSI-CARD.
3. Blank sheets of loose leaf paper can be put inside portfolio for journal writing.
4. As a music activity, invite students to design the front cover of the portfolio. Following are some options:
    - Create art that depicts what music "looks like" as it is being heard.
    - Design the musical instrument that "forgot to get invented."
    - Illustrate a variety of musical symbols and terms.
    - Conduct a timed contest: student with the longest list on his/her portfolio cover of all the places where music can be heard, wins a prize.

As a music activity, invite students to design the front cover of the portfolio.

Sample
STUDENT MUSIC PORTFOLIO

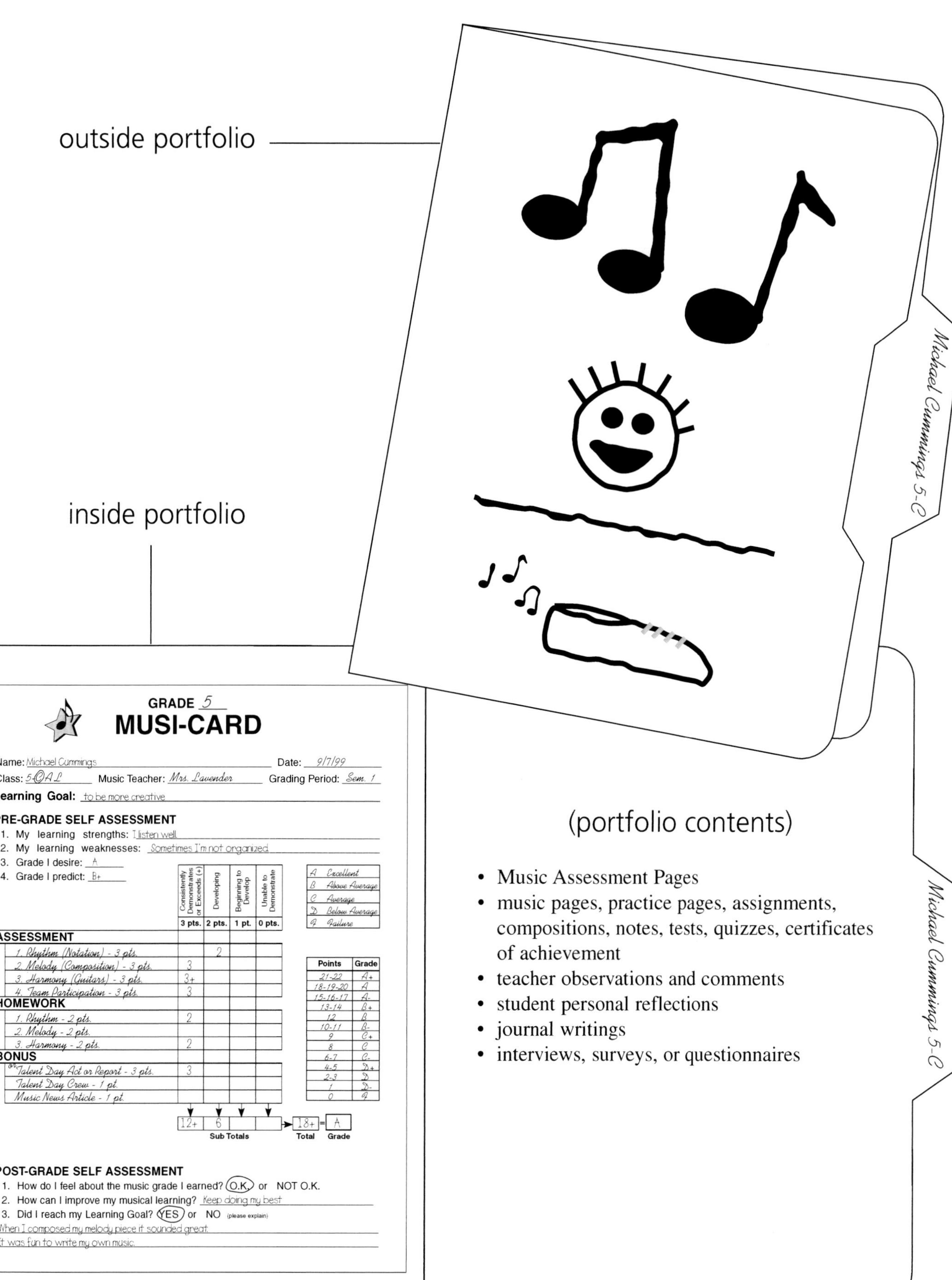

outside portfolio
Michael Cummings 5-C
inside portfolio
Michael Cummings 5-C
(portfolio contents)
• Music Assessment Pages
• music pages, practice pages, assignments, compositions, notes, tests, quizzes, certificates of achievement
• teacher observations and comments
• student personal reflections
• journal writings
• interviews, surveys, or questionnaires

GRADE 5

MUSI-CARD

Name: Michael Cummings Date: 9/7/99

Class: 5-©AL Music Teacher: Mrs. Lavender Grading Period: Sem. 1

Learning Goal: to be more creative

PRE-GRADE SELF ASSESSMENT

1. My learning strengths: I listen well.
2. My learning weaknesses: Sometimes I'm not organized
3. Grade I desire: A
4. Grade I predict: B+

	Consistently Demonstrates or Exceeds (+)	Developing	Beginning to Develop	Unable to Demonstrate
	3 pts.	2 pts.	1 pt.	0 pts.
ASSESSMENT				
1. Rhythm (Notation) - 3 pts.		2		
2. Melody (Composition) - 3 pts.	3			
3. Harmony (Guitars) - 3 pts.	3+			
4. Team Participation - 3 pts.	3			
HOMEWORK				
1. Rhythm - 2 pts.	2			
2. Melody - 2 pts.				
3. Harmony - 2 pts.	2			
BONUS				
or Talent Day Act or Report - 3 pts.	3			
Talent Day Crew - 1 pt.				
Music News Article - 1 pt.				
Sub Totals	12+	6		

Total: 18+ = Grade: A

A	Excellent
B	Above Average
C	Average
D	Below Average
F	Failure

Points	Grade
21-22	A+
18-19-20	A
15-16-17	A-
13-14	B+
12	B
10-11	B-
9	C+
8	C
6-7	C-
4-5	D+
2-3	D
1	D-
0	F

POST-GRADE SELF ASSESSMENT

1. How do I feel about the music grade I earned? (O.K.) or NOT O.K.
2. How can I improve my musical learning? Keep doing my best
3. Did I reach my Learning Goal? (YES) or NO (please explain)

When I composed my melody piece it sounded great.

It was fun to write my own music.

NINE NATIONAL STANDARDS FOR MUSIC EDUCATION

Music Content Standards

1. ***Singing alone and with others, a varied repertoire of music***

2. ***Performing on instruments, alone and with others, a varied repertoire of music***

3. ***Improvising melodies, variations, and accompaniments***

4. ***Composing and arranging music within specified guidelines***

5. ***Reading and notating music***

6. ***Listening to, analyzing, and describing music***

7. ***Evaluating music and music performance***

8. ***Understanding relationships between music, the other arts, and disciplines outside the arts***

9. ***Understanding music in relation to history and culture***

The above Music Content Standards are taken from *National Standards For Arts Education* (What Every Young American Should Know and Be Able to Do in the Arts), developed by the Consortium of National Arts Education Association, published by MENC, Reston, VA, 1994. The Music Content Standards are divided into three grade level categories: K-4; 5-8; and 9-12. Included with each Music Content Standard are numerous Achievement Standards that describe specific musical tasks with guidelines for competency.

Name: ______________________________________ Date: __________
Class: __________ Music Teacher: ________________ Grading Period: _______

GRADE _____

MUSIC ASSESMENT # __________

Concept: ____________________________________

Music Standard
or Learner Objective: ____________________________________

A TASK (check √)

Self Assessor: ______________________________

❑ ❑ ____

❑ ❑ ____

❑ ❑ ____

*If student is unable to participate with appropriate musical team behavior, assessment score is lowered one point.

B ASSESSMENT

At this time the learner…

- ❑ **3+** *exceeds*
- ❑ **3** *consistently demonstrates*
- ❑ **2** *is developing*
- ❑ **1** *is beginning to develop*
- ❑ **0** *is unable to demonstrate*

…competency at the task with meaningful, musical understanding.

C REFLECTION

____

____

____

____

____

____

____

GRADE ____

MUSI-CARD

Name: ____ Date: _______________

Class: _____________ Music Teacher: __________________ Grading Period: ________

MUSI-CARD

Cut outs

Learning Goal: ______________________________

PRE-GRADE SELF ASSESSMENT

1. My learning strengths: ______________________________
2. My learning weaknesses: ______________________________
3. Grade I desire: _______
4. Grade I predict: _______

POST-GRADE SELF ASSESSMENT

1. How do I feel about the music grade I earned? O.K. or NOT O.K.
2. How can I improve my musical learning? ______________________________
3. Did I reach my Learning Goal? YES or NO (please explain)

____

____

MUSI-CARD

Cut outs

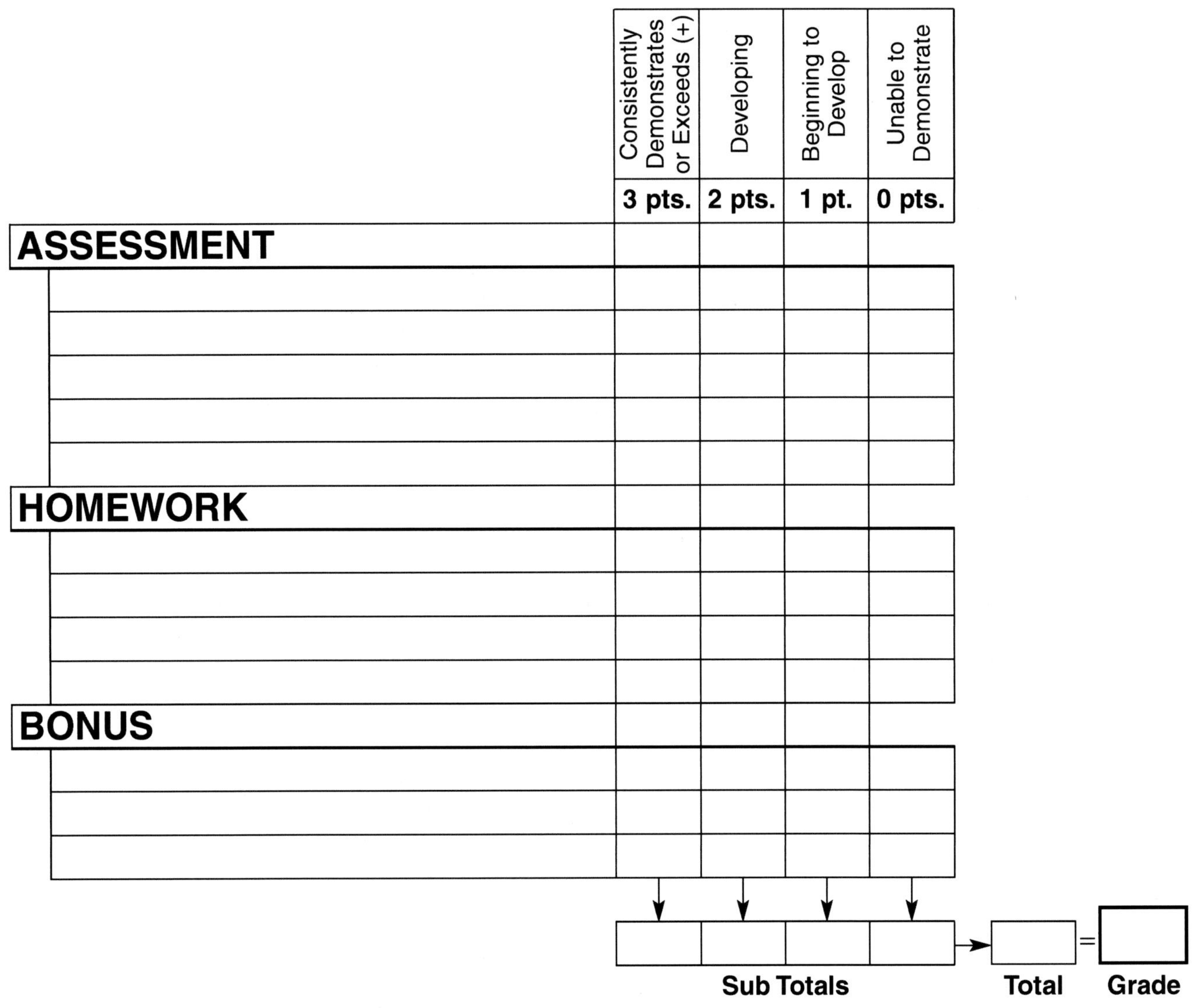

	Consistently Demonstrates or Exceeds (+)	Developing	Beginning to Develop	Unable to Demonstrate
	3 pts.	2 pts.	1 pt.	0 pts.
ASSESSMENT				
HOMEWORK				
BONUS				

Sub Totals → Total = Grade

Points	Grade

Points	Grade

Points	Grade

Points	Grade

Points	Grade

MUSI-CARD

Cut outs

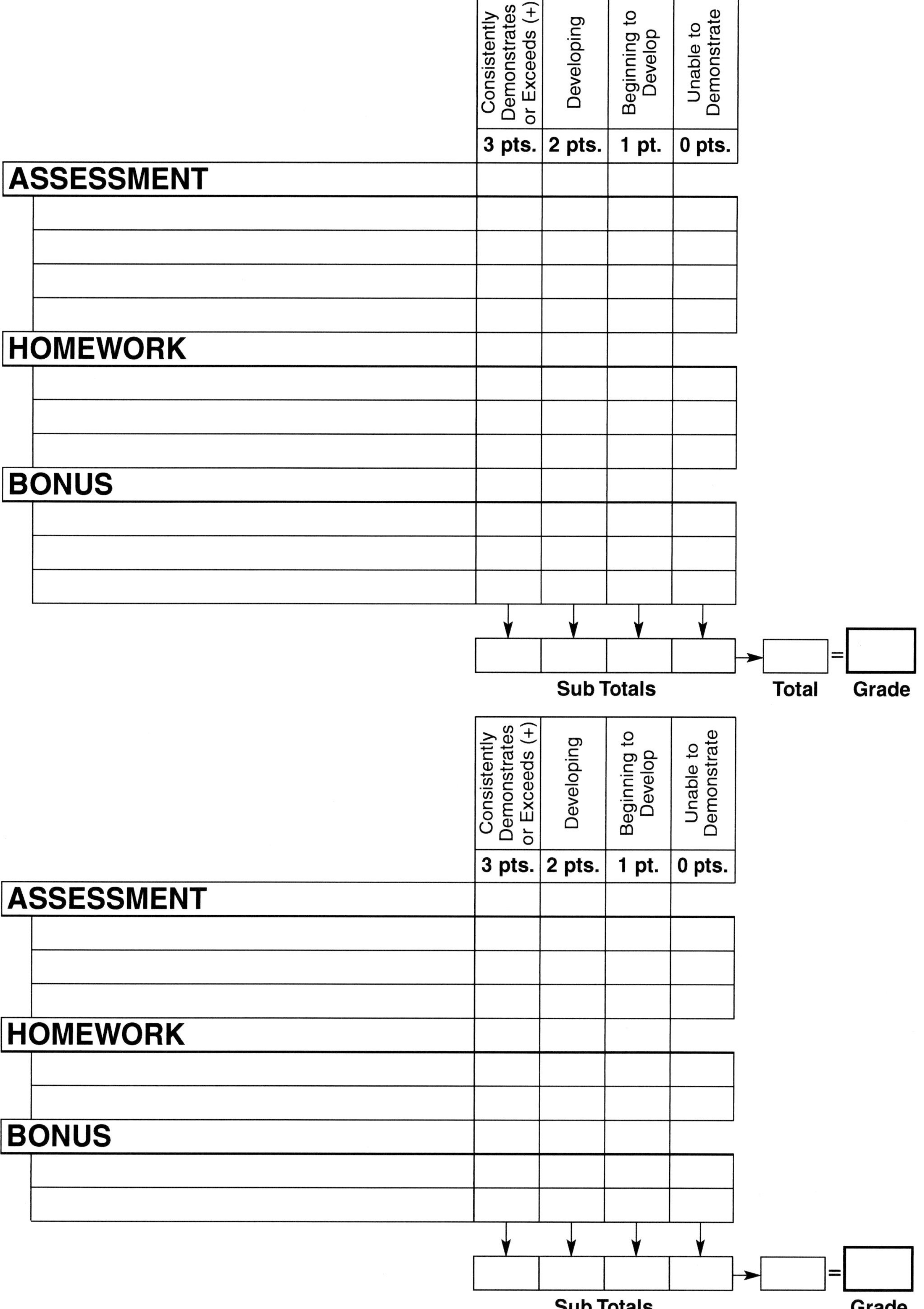

	Consistently Demonstrates or Exceeds (+)	Developing	Beginning to Develop	Unable to Demonstrate
	3 pts.	2 pts.	1 pt.	0 pts.
ASSESSMENT				
HOMEWORK				
BONUS				

Sub Totals → Total = Grade

	Consistently Demonstrates or Exceeds (+)	Developing	Beginning to Develop	Unable to Demonstrate
	3 pts.	2 pts.	1 pt.	0 pts.
ASSESSMENT				
HOMEWORK				
BONUS				

Sub Totals → = Grade

MUSI-CARD

Cut outs

ASSESSMENT	Consistently Demonstrates or Exceeds (+) 3 pts.	Developing 2 pts.	Beginning to Develop 1 pt.	Unable to Demonstrate 0 pts.

ASSESSMENT	Consistently Demonstrates or Exceeds (+) 3 pts.	Developing 2 pts.	Beginning to Develop 1 pt.	Unable to Demonstrate 0 pts.

ASSESSMENT	Consistently Demonstrates or Exceeds (+) 3 pts.	Developing 2 pts.	Beginning to Develop 1 pt.	Unable to Demonstrate 0 pts.

ASSESSMENT	Consistently Demonstrates or Exceeds (+) 3 pts.	Developing 2 pts.	Beginning to Develop 1 pt.	Unable to Demonstrate 0 pts.

ASSESSMENT	Consistently Demonstrates or Exceeds (+) 3 pts.	Developing 2 pts.	Beginning to Develop 1 pt.	Unable to Demonstrate 0 pts.

MUSI-CARD

Cut outs

HOMEWORK				

HOMEWORK				

HOMEWORK				

HOMEWORK				

BONUS				

BONUS				

BONUS				

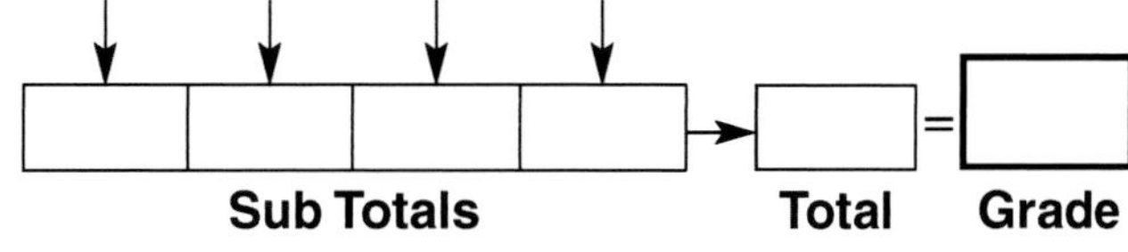

RESOURCES

Consortium of National Arts Education Associations. *National Standards for Arts Education.* Reston, VA: MENC, 1994.

Gardner, Howard. "The ArtsPROPEL Approach to Education in the Arts." *Kodaly Envoy,* Volume XX, No.2. Winter, 1994.

Gardner, Howard. *The Disciplined Mind: What All Students Should Understand.* New York: Simon and Schuster, 1999

Gardner, Howard. Project Zero. (Online) March, 2000. http://www.pz.harvard.edu/

Lehman, Paul R. "Assessment and Grading." *Teaching Music.* December, 1997. Reston, VA: MENC

Lehman, Paul R. "Grading Practices In Music." *Music Educators Journal.* March 1998. Reston, VA: MENC.

MENC. *Performance Standards for Music: Strategies and Benchmarks for Assessing Progress Toward the National Standards, Grades PreK-12.* Reston, VA: MENC, 1996.

Robinson, Mitchell. "Alternative Assessment Techniques for Teachers." *Music Educators Journal.* Volume 81, No. 5. March, 1995. Reston, VA: MENC.

Shuler, Scott C. "Assessment in General Music: Trends and Innovations in Local, State, and National Assessment." *In Toward Tomorrow: New Visions for General Music.* Reston, VA: MENC, 1995.

Shuler, Scott C. "The Effects of the National Standards on Assessment (and Vice Versa)." In *Aiming For Excellence: The Impact of the Standards Movement on Music Education.* Reston, VA: MENC, 1996.

Sousa, David. *How The Brain Learns.* Reston. VA: The National Association of Secondary School Principals, 1995

Winner, E., Davidson, L., & Scripp, L. (Ed). 1992. *ArtsPROPEL: A Handbook For Music.* Cambridge, MA.: Educational Testing Service and Project Zero.